The Heart
and Circulation

Carol Ballard

KIDHAVEN PRESS
An imprint of Thomson Gale, a part of The Thomson Corporation

Detroit • New York • San Francisco • San Diego • New Haven, Conn. • Waterville, Maine • London • Munich

Produced by Arcturus Publishing Ltd,
26/27 Bickels Yard, 151–153 Bermondsey Street, London SE1 3HA

© 2005 Arcturus Publishing

The right of Carol Ballard to be identified as the author of this work has been asserted by her in accordance with the Copyright, Designs and Patents Act 1988.

Series concept: Alex Woolf
Editor: Alex Woolf
Designer: Peta Morey
Artwork: Michael Courtney
Picture researcher: Glass Onion Pictures
Consultant: Dr Kristina Routh

Thomson and Star Logo are trademarks and Gale and KidHaven Press are registered trademarks used herein under license.

For more information, contact
KidHaven Press
27500 Drake Rd.
Farmington Hills, MI 48331-3535
Or you can visit our Internet site at http://www.gale.com

Picture Credits
Science Photo Library: 5 (Scott Camazine, Sue Trainor), 7 (Zephyr), 11 (Mauro Fermariello), 13 (Susan Kuklin), 15 (Ouellette & Theroux, Publiphoto Diffusion), 16 (Martin Riedl), 17 (Zephyr), 18 (Zephyr), 19 (James King-Holmes), 21 (Mark Clarke), 22 (David Scharf), 24 (Antonia Reeve), 25 (Sam Ogden), 26 (Antonia Reeve), 27 (Tek Image), 28 (Dr Gopal Murti), 29 (Alex Bartel).

LIBRARY OF CONGRESS CATALOGING-IN-PUBLICATION DATA

Ballard, Carol.
    The heart and circulation / by Carol Ballard.
        p. cm. — (Exploring the human body)
    Includes bibliographical references and index.
    ISBN 0-7377-3019-6 (hardcover : alk. paper)
    1. Cardiovascular system—Juvenile literature. I. Title. II. Series.
    QP103.B356 2005
    612.1—dc22
                                                    2004023216

Printed in Singapore

Contents

Introduction

Your heart is one of the most important organs in your body. It beats every minute of every day of your life, whether you are awake or asleep, sitting still or running around. You never have to think about making your heart beat. It just does it automatically.

Your heart is inside your chest, protected by the bones of your rib cage and surrounded and cushioned by your lungs. A network of tubes called blood vessels links the heart to the lungs. Another network of blood vessels connects the heart to the rest of the body.

Your heart is a strong pump made of muscle. Every time it beats, it pushes blood around your body. Blood cannot move loose around inside the body. Instead, it travels through blood vessels. In the same way that there are different types of roads such as freeways, side roads, and country lanes, there are also different types of blood vessels. Blood flows through the blood vessels in a one-way system, always moving in the same direction.

The heart pushes blood along the networks of blood vessels, forcing it

This picture shows the position of the heart in the body.

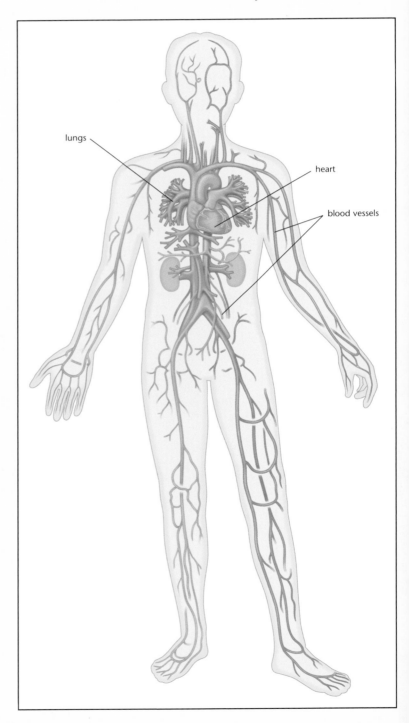

lungs

heart

blood vessels

around your body and eventually back to the heart again. Your blood travels around . . . and around . . . and around constantly, in a never-ending journey that is called blood circulation.

Sometimes your heart beats more quickly or more slowly than at other times. This is linked to how hard the rest of your body is working.

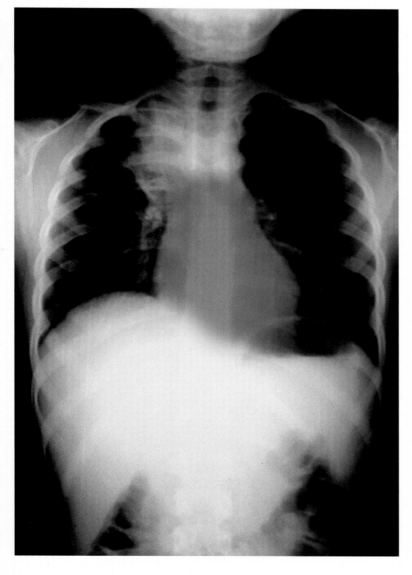

This X-ray shows the heart and lungs surrounded by the rib cage.

Like any other muscle, the heart needs to be strong to work well. This means that it needs regular exercise and a healthy diet. It is also important to avoid doing things that may damage your heart.

Case notes

Why does blood circulate?

Blood has several jobs to do. It is your body's transport system for oxygen and food, and it defends your body against germs. It helps control the amounts of water and chemicals in your body, and your body's temperature. To do these things it has to reach every part of your body. If your blood did not circulate, it would not be able to carry out all of its functions, which help keep you alive and healthy.

Blood Circulation

Blood has to reach every part of your body in order to carry out its functions of transport, control, and defense. It flows around your body through a network of tubes called blood vessels.

There are two networks of blood vessels. One carries blood from the right side of your heart to your lungs.

As you breathe in, your lungs fill up with air. Oxygen from the air moves into the blood. The blood, now with lots of oxygen in it, travels back to the left side of your heart for pumping to the rest of the body.

A waste gas called carbon dioxide, which is produced by other organs and muscles, moves out of the blood into the lungs. It leaves your body when you breathe out.

The other network of blood vessels carries blood from the left side of your heart to the rest of your body. As it passes through your organs and muscles, blood supplies them with oxygen. Your blood also collects waste carbon dioxide produced by organs and muscles. Blood travels back along the blood vessels to the right side of the heart, then to the lungs, then to the left side of the heart, then to the organs and muscles, then to the right side of the heart, and on and on in a never-ending journey!

Blood flows around the body in two networks of blood vessels. This diagram has been drawn as though you are looking in a mirror.

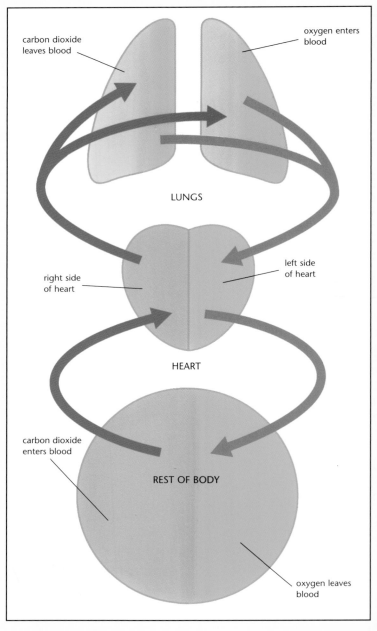

carbon dioxide leaves blood

oxygen enters blood

LUNGS

right side of heart

left side of heart

HEART

carbon dioxide enters blood

REST OF BODY

oxygen leaves blood

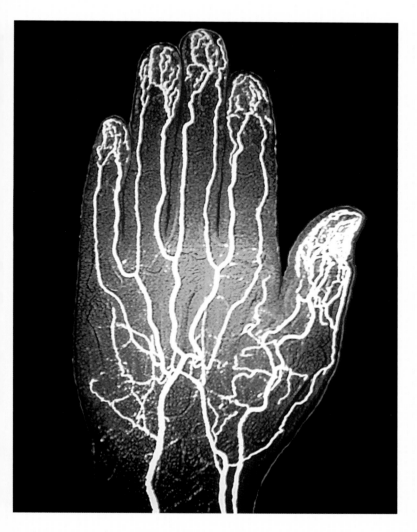

This X-ray shows some of the blood vessels in a hand.

Blood travels through blood vessels to every living part of your body, even to the very tips of your fingers and toes. Blood does not just carry oxygen and carbon dioxide, though. It carries other things too. Nutrients from your food are absorbed from your digestive system and taken to organs and muscles that need them. Waste chemicals and excess water are collected and taken away. These are removed from the blood by the liver and kidneys.

As it circulates, your blood also helps keep your body free from germs and anything else that may make you ill. Whenever you are awake or asleep, active or resting, this amazing network helps make sure that every part of your body has everything it needs to work properly.

Case notes

How many blood vessels are in my body?

There are blood vessels in every living part of your body. If you took an average adult's blood vessels and laid them all out in a straight line, they would stretch about 62,000 miles (100,000km)—that's long enough to go twice around the Earth and still have some left over!

The Heart

Your heart is a strong, muscular organ. It contracts and relaxes to pump blood around your body. It beats constantly, without your having to think about it or control it.

Your heart is roughly the same size and shape as your fist, but with a flattened top and a slightly pointed bottom. It is tipped a little to one side, with the bottom pointing toward your left.

Just like every other muscle in your body, your heart needs a constant supply of oxygen and nutrients. Waste products made by the heart muscle also have to be removed. To do this, your heart has its own special blood vessels carrying oxygen to it and carrying away its waste. These are called the coronary arteries and veins. They form a network around the outside of the heart, so that blood can reach every part of it.

Other large blood vessels lead into and out of the heart. The pulmonary artery carries blood from the heart to the lungs and the pulmonary vein carries blood from the lungs back to the heart. The aorta carries blood from the heart to the body and the venae cavae carry blood from the body back to the heart.

Here you can see the heart and its blood vessels.

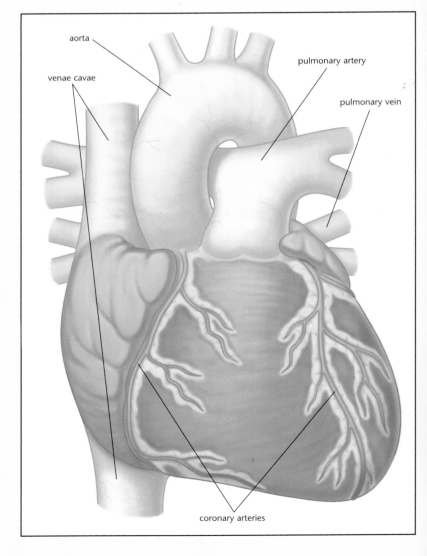

aorta

venae cavae

pulmonary artery

pulmonary vein

coronary arteries

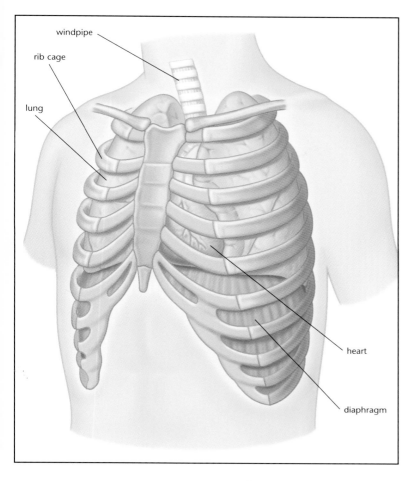

windpipe

rib cage

lung

heart

diaphragm

The heart lies inside the chest, protected by the bones of the rib cage.

The muscle that makes up your heart is called cardiac muscle. Although it is similar to the muscles in your arms and legs, there are some important differences. One is that if you damage a muscle in your arm or leg, it will heal and new muscle tissue will be made (although the muscle may not be as strong as it was before.) If cardiac muscle is damaged, only scar tissue is made. Another difference is that cardiac muscle itself partly controls when it contracts, but other muscles can only contract when signaled by the brain.

The heart itself has an outer layer called the pericardium, which protects the heart. It is anchored to the diaphragm below and the breastbone in front by strong fibers, so your heart is held firmly in place. The pericardium also produces a fluid that lubricates the heart so that it can move freely as it beats.

Case notes

How big is my heart?

Your heart has a mass of about 7 ounces (200g)—roughly the same as a large potato. Your heart grows along with the rest of your body, so an adult's heart is bigger and heavier than a child's.

Inside the Heart

Your heart is a pump made from strong, muscular walls with four spaces inside. These spaces are called chambers. A strong wall called the septum separates the chambers on the right from those on the left. This prevents blood in the left side from mixing with blood in the right side. The heart really operates as two separate pumps—one on each side.

The right side pumps blood to the lungs. The left side pumps blood to the rest of the body. The upper chambers on each side are called atria (the plural of atrium). The lower chambers are called ventricles.

Blood flows through the heart in a one-way system. This is controlled by strong flaps called valves. These open to let blood flow through them. They then snap shut to keep the blood from flowing back. The system is like a set of doors. One opens to let people into a room, then shuts when the room is full. Another opens at the other end of the room to let people out. When the room is empty, the first door opens again to let more people in—and so on. This way, the heart always has exactly the right amount of blood and can work well.

This diagram shows the internal structure of the heart.

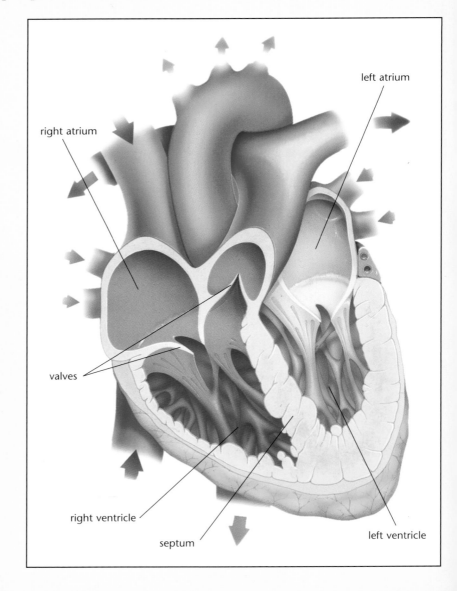

right atrium

left atrium

valves

right ventricle

septum

left ventricle

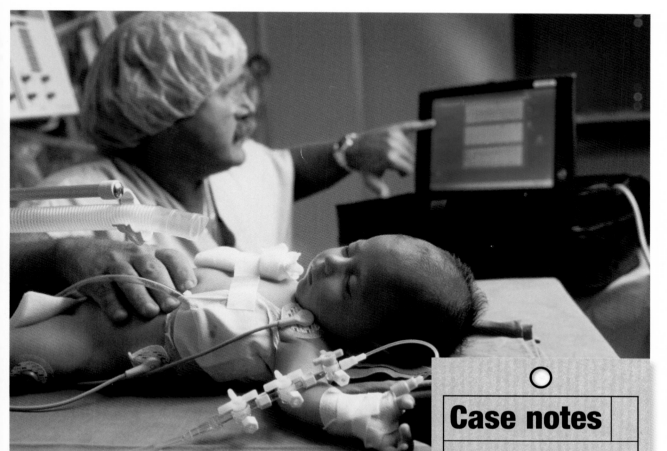

This baby is being monitored after heart surgery.

In some people, the valves do not close properly. They may have been faulty at birth, or damaged later by an illness. This means that some blood flows backward into the heart, so it works less well. As the blood flows backward, it makes a gurgling sound that doctors can hear and figure out exactly what is wrong. Doctors can replace damaged or faulty valves. The first replacement valves were from animals such as pigs. Today valves are made of metal or plastic. New valves make the heart work properly again.

Case notes

What is a "hole in the heart"?

The septum separates the right side of the heart from the left side. This keeps blood from moving straight across from one side to the other. In some babies, this wall is not formed properly, so there is a small gap between the two sides. This is a "hole in the heart." Blood can spill through, making the baby very ill. Doctors can operate to close the hole and make the baby well again.

Heartbeat

Every time your heart beats, it pushes blood through your blood vessels. Imagine a squeeze bottle filled with liquid, with a single tube attached to either end of the bottle. The bottle is like your heart, the tube is like your blood vessels, and the liquid is like your blood. If you squeeze the bottle, the liquid will be forced out of the bottle, along the tube and back into the other end of the bottle. This is just how your heart works: it squeezes to force blood out of the heart, through the blood vessels and back to the heart again.

The heartbeat sounds that you hear are made by the valves as they snap shut. There are two sounds to each heartbeat—lub-dup . . . lub-dup . . . lub-dup—as the two pairs of valves shut one after the other.

Each heartbeat has four stages:

1. The atria fill with blood.
2. The atria contract, pushing the blood against the valves. This forces the valves open, allowing blood to rush into the ventricles.
3. When the ventricles are full they contract and the valves between the atria and ventricles close to stop blood flowing backward. This makes the first "lub" sound of the heartbeat. The blood is then pushed against the next set of valves. These valves

This diagram shows the steps that take place in a single heartbeat.

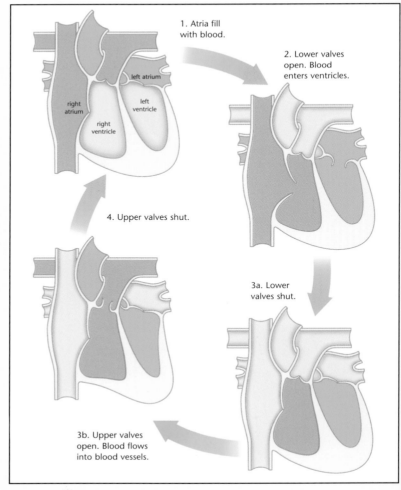

1. Atria fill with blood.

2. Lower valves open. Blood enters ventricles.

left atrium

right atrium

left ventricle

right ventricle

4. Upper valves shut.

3a. Lower valves shut.

3b. Upper valves open. Blood flows into blood vessels.

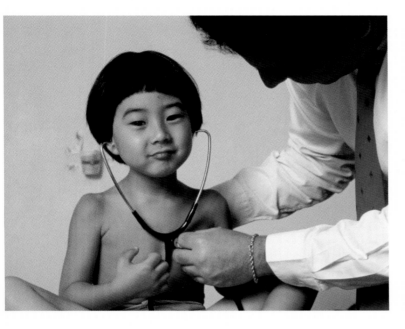

A stethoscope allows you to hear the sound of your heartbeat more clearly.

are forced open and blood is pushed out into the blood vessels.

4. The second set of valves shut, keeping the blood from flowing back into the ventricles. This makes the second "dup" sound of the heartbeat.

The whole sequence happens constantly, with the atria immediately filling with blood again as soon as the ventricles empty. Each heartbeat pumps about 2 ounces (70ml) of blood.

The walls of the ventricles are thicker and stronger than those of the atria. This is because only a gentle push is needed to pump blood from the atria into the ventricles. A much stronger push is needed to pump blood out of the ventricles and into the blood vessels.

Doctors often use an instrument called a stethoscope to listen to a patient's heart. This makes it easier for them to hear how well the heart is working. If they want more detailed information, they may use an electrocardiograph (ECG) machine. This detects and records electrical signals from the heart as it is beating. The results can be printed onto a chart or displayed on a screen.

Case notes

How can I feel my heart beating?

If you put your hand on the left side of your chest you may be able to feel your heart beating. You can also feel it by finding your pulse. Lay the index and middle finger of one hand gently on your other wrist, in a straight line with your thumb. You might be able to feel a beat. This is called your pulse. It is caused by the heart pumping blood along the arteries.

Exercise and Heart Rate

An adult's heart usually beats between seventy and eighty times every minute when the person is resting. Some people's hearts beat more quickly than this and others beat more slowly. Most children have a faster heartbeat than adults.

Your heart beats all the time. If it beats seventy times a minute, that's more than four thousand beats an hour . . . more than 100,000 beats a day . . . more than 35,000,000 beats a year! And that's just if you spend the whole year resting. If you run and exercise, it will be even more!

When you start to exercise, your heart starts to beat more quickly. This is because your muscles need more oxygen and more energy when they work hard than when

This graph shows how people's heart rates speed up when they exercise and slowly go back to their normal rates when they rest again.

These athletes exercise regularly so their hearts are fit and strong.

they are resting. They also produce waste more quickly, which needs to be removed. Your blood carries oxygen and nutrients to the muscles, and carries away waste products. To speed up the system, your heart has to pump faster.

When you stop exercising, your muscles need less oxygen and energy, and they make a smaller amount of waste. The blood has less to do, so it does not need to be pumped as quickly. Your heart gradually slows down and goes back to its normal resting rate.

Exercise makes your heart muscle stronger, which means that it works better. It can pump more blood with each beat, so it does not need to increase its rate very much when you exercise. It also goes back to normal more quickly when you stop exercising. Athletes who train and keep fit often have a much slower resting heart rate than people who do little exercise.

Your heart rate also speeds up if you get very excited or scared. Your body produces a special chemical that makes your heart beat more quickly. This is to keep you safe. If you were in danger and had to run away, your muscles would already have an extra supply of oxygen and energy.

Case notes

How are heart rate and breathing rate linked?

When you breathe in, oxygen passes from your lungs into your blood. Waste carbon dioxide moves out of your blood into your lungs and leaves your body when you breathe out. When you exercise, your muscles need more oxygen, so you need to breathe more quickly and deeply. Your heart then pumps more quickly to get the oxygen to your muscles. When you rest you need less oxygen, so the whole system slows down again.

Healthy Heart

Your heart is a very important organ, so it makes good sense to look after it as well as you can. There are several things you can do to keep your heart fit and healthy.

Exercise is good for your heart, just as it is for every other muscle in your body. Taking part in some regular exercise or sport makes your heart fitter and stronger. Activities such as dancing, swimming, cycling, team games, gymnastics, and horseback riding are all good for your heart. Many doctors recommend that you play sports or exercise at least four or five times a week.

Exercise like swimming is very good for your heart.

normal blood vessel

narrowed blood vessel

This X-ray shows damaged blood vessels. Blood cannot travel easily through the narrowed sections.

The food that you eat has a big effect on your whole body. Eating a balanced diet helps keep your body, including your heart, healthy. It also provides plenty of energy for exercise, work, and sports. It is important to eat something from each of these groups of foods every day:

- fresh fruit and vegetables—for vitamins and minerals
- whole-grain bread, pasta, rice, or other cereals—for energy
- meats, fish, eggs, and nuts—for protein

Sweet, sugary foods and fatty foods can taste great but they are not very good for your body. Try to think of these as treats. Enjoy them now and then but try to avoid eating too much of them.

Smoking cigarettes is really bad for your heart. Some of the chemicals in cigarette smoke can make your blood vessels narrower so your heart has to work extra hard to push the blood through them. This puts an extra strain on the heart and can lead to heart disease and serious damage.

Case notes

Does being overweight affect my heart?

Your heart has to pump blood all through your body. Being overweight can make this more difficult. The pressure of the blood in the blood vessels often increases, so every time your heart beats it has to give a harder push. Also, the heart has to pump blood to all the extra fat tissue in the body. Overall, being overweight puts an extra strain on your heart, making it harder for it to work properly and eventually damaging it.

Heart Attacks

The body needs the constant supply of oxygen, energy, and nutrients brought by the blood. It also needs the blood to carry away its waste products.

A heart attack is most often caused by a blockage in the coronary blood vessels. This prevents blood from reaching part of the heart muscle. Without fresh blood, this part of the heart dies. This affects the whole heart and stops it from beating properly. Without medical treatment, the patient may die.

In men, the first sign of a heart attack is often a severe chest pain. Women often have no chest pain, but feel sick and very tired. The victim's left hand and arm often tingle too, and he or she may find it hard to breathe. The sooner the person receives treatment, the better his or her chances of making a full recovery. By giving the person the right medicine as soon as possible, medical teams can relieve the pain and prevent any more damage to the heart. Medicines can often help remove the blockage in the coronary vessels.

A scan like this helps doctors to monitor the heart following a heart attack.

If the heart has completely stopped beating, or is just twitching instead of beating normally, defibrillation equipment can be used. This gives the heart an electric shock and can make it start to beat properly again. Mouth-to-mouth resuscitation and chest massage may help keep blood flowing through the body until the heart starts beating again.

After a heart attack, a person usually needs to spend some time recovering in the hospital. Doctors will usually carry

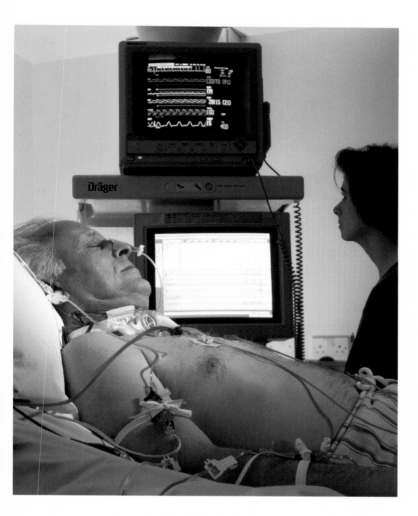

This heart attack patient is recovering in the hospital.

out tests to see how badly damaged the heart is. This will help them to decide what treatment is best for the person.

An operation to improve the coronary blood flow may be necessary. Heart attack patients are also advised to improve their lifestyle to avoid increasing the risk of another heart attack. This usually means eating a healthy, low-fat diet, getting plenty of exercise, and not smoking cigarettes.

The risk of having a heart attack is highest for people who smoke cigarettes, are very overweight, get little exercise, eat fatty diets, or have very stressful lives. Some diseases, such as diabetes, can increase the risk of a heart attack. Doctors also think that a person's genes may be involved, too, because heart attacks seem to be more common in some families than in others.

Case notes

What should I do in an emergency?

If you are alone with someone who you think may be having a heart attack, the most important thing is not to panic. If there is an adult nearby who you think you can trust, ask him or her for help. If not, find a telephone and dial 911 for emergency services. Tell the operator who you are and what the problem is. Listen carefully, answer any questions, and then follow any instructions you are given.

Blood Vessels

Blood vessels are the tubes through which blood travels from the heart to the rest of your body. Different blood vessels do different jobs, so they have different structures. There are three main types of blood vessels: arteries, veins, and capillaries.

Arteries These carry blood away from the heart. Every time the heart beats, blood is forced out into the arteries under high pressure. Arteries have strong, muscular walls so that they can stand up to this pressure. The artery walls are made up of a thick outer layer, a middle layer of muscles and fibers, and a thin inner lining. The walls are flexible and stretchy.

Veins These carry blood back to the heart. The blood is under less pressure than it is in the arteries, so the walls of the veins do not need to be as strong as artery walls. The outer and inner layers of the vein walls are like those of arteries, but the middle layer is thinner and has fewer muscles.

Veins have valves that keep blood from flowing backward. As blood moves toward the heart, it pushes the valves open. If blood starts to flow away from the heart, it pushes the valves shut.

Capillaries To make a complete network, arteries and veins must be linked together. Arteries branch into narrower tubes. These branch again and again, getting

These diagrams show the inner structures of arteries, veins, and capillaries.

outer layer
strong muscular layer
lining
ARTERY

outer layer
VEIN
valve
weak muscular layer
lining

CAPILLARY
thin wall

narrower every time. Eventually they branch into the narrowest blood vessels, the capillaries. The capillaries carry blood through the tissues of the body and then join together again, making larger blood vessels. These join again and again, eventually making veins.

Capillaries form very fine networks throughout the body. The walls of capillaries are so thin that gases and chemicals can pass through them. This means that nutrients and oxygen can move out of the blood in the capillaries and into the body tissues where they are needed. Also, carbon dioxide and other waste products can move out of the body tissues and into the capillaries and be carried away by the blood.

Some capillaries lie very close to the surface of your skin. When you are hot, lots of blood flows through these capillaries. This helps you to lose heat through your skin. The blood flowing close to the surface makes your skin look red. When you are cold, the opposite happens. Less blood flows through the skin's capillaries, so less heat is lost, and your skin looks pale.

Blood flowing through the skin's capillaries makes this child's face look red, and helps him cool down.

Blood

Blood is your body's internal transport system and it defends your body against germs. It helps control the amounts of water and chemicals in your body, and also helps to control your body's temperature. A single drop of blood contains millions and millions of tiny cells in a watery liquid.

These red blood cells have been photographed under a microscope.

Red blood cells are like discs that have been squashed at the top and bottom. They are tiny. You would need about 125 side by side to make a line about four-hundredths of an inch (1mm) long! Red blood cells carry oxygen throughout your body. It is their color that makes your blood look red.

White blood cells can be all sorts of shapes and sizes. They are your body's defense system. Some release special chemicals to destroy germs such as bacteria and viruses. Some surround any particles that should not be in your body and destroy them. Some develop a chemical "memory" of germs so that they can attack them quickly the next time they find them.

Platelets are very, very tiny fragments of cells. They help your blood to clot and form a scab.

Plasma is the watery liquid that all your blood cells float around in. It contains many different chemicals and nutrients that it carries to every part of your body. Waste chemicals are also carried in the plasma until they are removed by the liver or kidneys.

Blood cells are made in your bone marrow, the soft material at the center of some bones. Some travel to other parts of your body to finish developing. Some white blood cells only live for a day or two. Others may live for two or three months, while a very few may live for more than a year. Red blood cells live for about three months. At the end of their life, blood cells are destroyed by your spleen and liver. Some of the chemicals they were made from are stored or reused, while others leave the body in your urine.

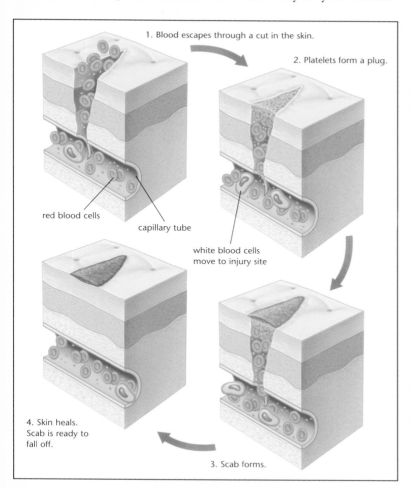

1. Blood escapes through a cut in the skin.

2. Platelets form a plug.

red blood cells

capillary tube

white blood cells move to injury site

4. Skin heals. Scab is ready to fall off.

3. Scab forms.

Platelets help a scab to form over a cut.

Case notes

What happens when I cut myself?

When you cut yourself, blood oozes out of the cut skin. Unless the cut is very deep, the blood soon stops flowing. It becomes sticky and eventually a scab forms over the surface of the cut. The platelets in your blood contain special chemicals to make the blood stick together, or clot. They also make a mesh to cover the cut and form a scab. Below this, the cut heals as new skin is made. When the cut is completely healed, the scab falls off. If you pick at a scab, you may damage the new skin that is forming beneath it.

Blood Types

Although humans are alike in many ways, we are also different in other ways. For example, although we have two arms, a head, and ten toes, you may be tall or short, have black hair or blond hair, brown eyes or blue eyes. In the same way, we all have red blood cells but they may have different chemicals on their surfaces. Using these red blood cell differences, scientists put blood into different types.

The main blood type system is called ABO. This system was created in 1930 by Karl Landsteiner, an American scientist. The name comes from two special chemicals, A and B, that may be on your red blood cells. These chemicals determine your ABO blood type. The following table shows how this works:

A scientist carries out a test on some donated blood to see which type it is.

Blood type	Chemical on blood cells
A	A
B	B
AB	A and B
O	neither A nor B

If blood of different types is mixed together, one type can react against the other. This would make you very ill.

Most of the time your blood type makes no difference to you at all. However, doctors may need to know your blood type before you have an operation. They can find this out by doing a simple blood test to see which of the chemicals A and B your blood contains.

Another important blood type is the rhesus type. This was first discovered in rhesus monkeys. People whose blood contains a chemical called rhesus factor are blood

The rhesus factor was discovered in rhesus monkeys like this one.

type rhesus positive (Rh+). Those whose blood does not contain the rhesus factor are blood type rhesus negative (Rh-).

ABO and rhesus blood types are usually referred to together. For example, someone might say they are "AB+," meaning their ABO type is AB and they are Rh+.

Giving blood from an Rh- person to an Rh+ person causes no problems, but giving Rh+ blood to an Rh- person can make them very ill. If an Rh+ mother is expecting an Rh- baby, her blood can harm the baby. Doctors can now check this before the baby is born and give the mother an injection to prevent any problems for the baby.

Case notes

What is a blood transfusion?

If we cut ourselves, we may lose a small amount of blood, but this is not likely to do any harm. However, it can be dangerous to lose a lot of blood, either through a serious accident or because of a surgical operation. Doctors may use blood from a blood donor to replace the lost blood. This transfer of blood from one person to another is called a blood transfusion. It is important that the blood types of patient and donor are known and matched so that the patient does not receive blood that their own blood will react against.

Giving Blood

A constant supply of blood is needed because there is a never-ending list of people who need blood transfusions. Doctors like to have a supply of blood available to replace any blood that might be lost during a major operation. Also, people who suffer serious accidents may need blood to replace what they have lost. Patients with some illnesses, such as leukemia and anemia, may also need to be given blood. Doctors can never know how many people will need blood, or when they will need it, so it is safest to make sure there is always plenty available.

Giving blood is safe and may help to save another person's life.

Not everybody is allowed to give blood. Different countries have different rules, but in most countries you have to be over a certain age. Until you are fully grown, it might harm your body if you give blood. Some countries also have an upper age limit.

To give blood, people go to a blood donation center. Some centers are in hospitals or separate clinics, but others are in mobile units. Mobile units travel around so that it is as easy as possible for people to get to them and give blood.

Before a person gives blood, he or she is asked lots of questions and a small sample of his or her blood is tested. This is to check that it is safe for that person to give his or

Donated blood is often stored in large refrigerators like this one.

her blood. When everything is ready, the donor sits or lies on a special chair or bed. A sterile needle is put into a vein at the inside of his or her elbow, and a collecting bag is attached to the other end of the needle via a plastic tube. Blood flows out of the vein, down the tube, and into the bag. When enough has been collected, the donor rests quietly for a while and then leaves.

Blood is stored at blood banks. Donated blood may be refrigerated and stored as whole blood. It is often separated, though, and red blood cells, white blood cells, platelets, and plasma are each stored separately. One patient may need plasma and another red blood cells, for example, so one blood donation can be used to treat more than one person.

Case notes

How do we know donated blood is safe?

Whenever a person gives blood, the blood is tested to find out which type it is. It is also tested to make sure that it does not contain any viruses or anything else that might harm a patient to whom the blood is given. As scientists discover more about diseases, they are able to carry out more advanced tests to check that the donated blood is safe.

Blood Problems

Most people have healthy blood that does not cause them many problems. There are some blood disorders, though, that can cause serious problems.

Hemophilia This is an inherited condition, much more common in males than females, that prevents the blood from clotting properly. People with hemophilia bruise very easily and it is very difficult to stop the bleeding if they have a cut. In very bad cases, blood may leak into a child's joints, stopping them from forming properly and making them very painful. Until recently, doctors had no way of treating hemophilia. Now, though, it can be treated by regular injections of blood-clotting chemicals.

Sickle-cell anemia In this inherited disease, red blood cells lose their usual round shape and become stretched and twisted. These deformed red blood cells cannot carry as much oxygen as normal red blood cells, so the person feels tired and weak. These cells can also block blood vessels, causing pain, especially in joints and bones. Sickle-cell anemia can often be treated by

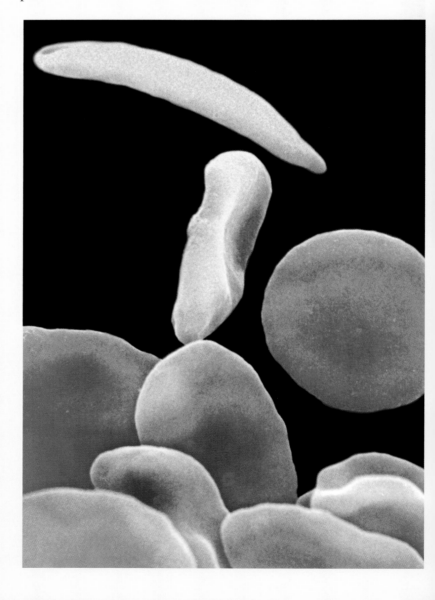

In sickle-cell anemia, red blood cells become deformed and twisted.

medicines. Sometimes a blood transfusion is needed to provide enough healthy red blood cells.

Sickle-cell anemia, and a milder form known as sickle-cell trait, are common in countries near the equator. Malaria, a disease carried by mosquitoes, is also common in these places. Scientists have found that having sickled blood cells makes the blood poisonous to these mosquitoes—so it protects against malaria!

Bruises can be sore but they soon heal.

Leukemia People with leukemia have too many white blood cells in their blood. This means that none of the white blood cells can develop and work properly, so the body cannot defend itself against infections. The extra white blood cells also stop the bone marrow from making red blood cells, so the blood's oxygen supply is affected, making the person feel tired and weak. Leukemia can be treated with special medicines (chemotherapy) and radiation (radiotherapy). Some patients may also receive a bone marrow transplant, often from a brother or sister.

Case notes

What is a bruise?

A bruise is usually the result of a knock or blow to the skin. This damages blood vessels in the skin, and blood leaks out of them. The surface of the skin is not damaged and so the blood cannot escape. Instead, it spreads out inside the skin and you see a dark mark—a bruise. This often has a dark, purple-blue color at first. After a few days, the color fades to yellow-green as the body breaks up the blood cells and clears them away. Eventually, the bruise vanishes completely.

Glossary

aorta — The main artery carrying blood away from the heart.

artery — One of the large blood vessels carrying blood away from the heart.

atrium — One of the upper chambers of the heart.

bacteria — A type of microorganism.

capillary — One of the tiniest blood vessels.

carbon dioxide — A waste gas produced by the body.

cardiac — Having to do with the heart.

circulation — The movement of blood through the body.

coronary — Having to do with the heart.

digestive system — Organs that break up and absorb your food.

germ — A microorganism that can cause illness.

inherited — Passed on from one generation to the next.

kidneys — Organs that remove waste salts and water from the blood.

liver — The organ that controls many chemical reactions in the body.

nutrients — The parts of your food that your body can use.

oxygen — A gas that every part of your body needs to stay alive.

pericardium — The outer covering of the heart.

plasma — The liquid part of the blood.

platelet — A tiny cell fragment that helps blood clot.

pulmonary — Having to do with the lungs.

red blood cell — The part of the blood that carries oxygen.

rib cage — Bones that form the chest and protect the heart and lungs.

septum — The central wall separating the two sides of the heart.

valve — A flap that controls the direction of blood flow.

vein — One of the blood vessels that carry blood back to the heart.

venae cavae — Main veins that carry blood back to the heart.

ventricle — One of the lower chambers of the heart.

virus — A microorganism that can cause illness.

white blood cell — The part of the blood that protects you from illness and infection.

For Further Exploration

Books

DK Guide to the Human Body
(Dorling Kindersley, 2004)

My Healthy Body: Blood and Heart
by Jen Green (Franklin Watts, 2003)

The Oxford Children's A to Z of the Human Body
by Bridget and Neil Ardley
(Oxford University Press, 2003)

Under the Microscope: Heart
by C. Gregory (Franklin Watts, 2001)

Usborne Internet-Linked Complete Book of the Human Body
by Anna Claybourne
(Usborne Publishing, 2003)

Web Sites

www.americanheart.org
click on "Children's Heart Health"

www.cyh.com
click on "health information just for kids,"
then type in "heart" in the search field

www.kidshealth.org/kid/body/heart_no5W.html
all about your heart

Index